ABOUT ORGANIC GARDENING

ABOUT ORGANIC GARDENING

by

G. J. BINDING M.B.E., F.R.H.S.

THORSONS PUBLISHERS LIMITED
37/38 Margaret Street, London, W.1

First published December 1970
Second Impression March 1972

ISBN 0 7225 0164 1

Made and Printed in Great Britain by
Weatherby Woolnough Ltd., Wellingborough
Northants, England

CONTENTS

INTRODUCTION

WHAT DO WE really mean by 'organic' in relation to the soil?
It is something much more important and far-reaching than
just not using artificial fertilizers, insecticides, and weed killers.
In simple terms that all lovers of the land will understand,
organic means natural cultivation. In our concrete multi-
storied cities of today, we can be as far away from nature as
the first man on the moon from the earth. Inside everyone is
an urge to return to the state of nature. The Yogis believed
we should get our hands into the soil as often as possible to
enable us to live in complete harmony.

One of the simplest ways of getting back to nature is to adopt
a system of organic gardening. It will bring a new and lasting
interest affecting our entire lives. The basis of all organic
gardening is a determined effort to increase the humus content
and fertility of the soil so that one may dispense entirely with
all chemical aids. There is no magic wand which can be waved
over the earth; no short cut to fertility with potions, powders or
other means. Fertile organic soils cannot be produced by the
scientist or chemist in any shape or form. Chemical fertilizers
have all the ingredients but lack vitality and life-giving properties. In the long run this results in an equally lifeless soil and
an increase in pests and diseases. The only way is by allowing
natural processes to develop by means of composting, something man can never imitate for it is brought about by an act
of God.

In organic composting the cycle is completed—without
exception all that came from the soil is returned in one form or
another. The only aid is the use of an organic activator which
will greatly, in fact, miraculously, increase the process of
decomposition. The action of natural composting has to be

7

seen to be believed; a process beyond the ability of man to
imitate; a natural act as mysterious as life itself. This natural
method is as old as the world, it does more than simply provide
health-giving crops, it keeps the balance of nature. All creatures, worms, insects, birds and other forms of wild life, down
to the tiniest microbes, are allowed to grow and play their
vital role in the cycle. They are either consumed by other species,
or allowed to die off, and in doing so, add a minute part to the
everlasting vegetable and organic mass, which in turn becomes
compost. In China, with the largest population of any country
in the world, the compost heap plays an important part in
the life of the community. The Chinese, ancient and modern, in
their very wise manner, have always maintained a fertile soil.

It is now over one hundred years since the discovery of the
artificial fertilizer. Over a century of so-called progress which
many now realize has meant the abuse of the soil and natural
resources. We have, during the last few decades, witnessed a
world-wide transformation of farming methods. Progress has
been made with automation and artificial fertilizing of soils
and crops. The scientist has come to the aid of the farmer,
small holder, market gardener and everyone of us in our little
gardens. All manner of pests may be quickly exterminated by
either spraying with a liquid insecticide, or applying it in powder form. The farmer with a large acreage can even employ a
light aircraft, piloted by an expert in the art of spraying crops.
There are as many chemicals used in the form of insecticides as
there are pests to combat. The scientist has provided everything we need, and artificial fertilizers have become part of
agricultural life for farmers and gardeners in most countries.
We must now take stock and see what these miraculous discoveries have really done to the farmlands of the world.
Lack of organic matter in soils results, in the long run, in
infertility and disaster, and after decades of misuse, arable
land becomes a desolate waste.

Our garden soil, nurseries, smallholdings and, most important of all, farmland, must be made so fertile that chemical
additives will not be needed. The simple and long term answer
to this problem lies in compost making. More and more com-

post obtained year in and year out, ripened by one of the many organic methods. For good crops, practically disease free, and full of vitality, we need black, rich soil containing humus and living organisms, unfortunately not often found on a large scale today. For those who really care about the world's agriculture, and this should be everyone, there is only one answer, the reintroduction of organic farming everywhere.

It is hoped that this little booklet will help resolve some of the problems you may have experienced in organic gardening. The only way to succeed is to start making compost; it is interesting, you have much to learn, but the results are worthwhile.

CHAPTER ONE

THE COMPOST HEAP

A TREND IN recent years of making the compost heap the heart and soul of the plot, garden, or farm, is becoming more evident. There are a variety of methods of compost making, all equally good, provided certain safeguards are taken. To understand something about the way organic matter disintegrates makes for more successful results.

Containers

An ideal receptacle for a compost heap is an old packing case. First drill a number of holes around it at six inch intervals, to allow ventilation slits to be cut in all four sides. The bottom must be removed from the case, but the lid can be retained for occasional use in preventing the heap becoming saturated during heavy rain. If the box has not been painted it should be treated with some preservative such as engine oil or Stockholm tar. Wood is the best material to use, it retains the warmth, is comparatively cheap, and if protected will last for many years. If a box is not available one will have to be constructed. The container should ideally be placed in a semi-shady position, not facing north. The contents must come into direct contact with the earth. If the soil beneath the proposed site is first dug over and some ripe compost introduced, worms will be encouraged to appear and assist the process of decomposition. Other materials which may be used for making containers include brick walls or asbestos sheets, provided spaces or slits are left for ventilation. Once constructed, every effort should be made to fill the container as quickly as possible. This makes for a quicker break-down into compost and aids the build up and retention of heat.

Building the Heap

A little attention to detail in constructing the heap makes for better results in the end. All kinds of vegetable waste may be used, including dead leaves from every vegetable or flower. Lawn mowings, hedge clippings, vegetable matter from the kitchen, including potato peelings, tea and coffee grounds, and egg shells, can all be composted. Contents of vacuum cleaners and carpet sweepers can also be used. Some people put kitchen meat wastage, such as bacon rind, on the heap, but this is not ideal for air will be excluded. Meat and fish scraps also encourage flies, mice, and cause smells. As a guide, anything that came from the soil may be returned.

On being constructed, each layer should be about four inches in depth. An attempt should be made to intersperse layers of stalks and tougher substances between sections of softer material such as lawn mowings. This aids the process of decomposition. Layers should be pressed down by hand and not trampled under foot; slight pressure is sufficient. If the heap is made too compact, air is excluded and it may putrify. This applies in particular to heaps which are made up of large amounts of softer components such as grass cuttings. Soil should be lightly scattered on top of every foot being built, and many add a light dusting of lime to the soil, but this is purely optional.

Use of the Activator

There are a number of ways in which an organic activator may be introduced into compost making to ensure speedy and successful decomposition. The writer has obtained excellent results from Miss Bruce's Quick Return organic compost activator. For the cost of 1s. 9d., sufficient ready prepared powder may be purchased to make up to two tons of the finest organic compost. Full directions for use are given with each packet. You simply obtain one pint of water (rain water being the best medium) place one teaspoonful of the powder into the water and allow it to stand for 24 hours. It then becomes a sweet smelling liquid which retains its strength for about four weeks. On becoming sour it should be discarded.

Methods of Application

The horizontal way: Assuming you have obtained the Quick Return activator from your local gardening shop, or direct by post from Chase Organics, mix a teaspoonful of the powder with a pint of rain water and allow it to stand for twenty-four hours. During the process of building the heap it should be activated by a light application of the solution on about every four-inch layer. Having applied the activator, immediately cover the heap with a further layer of fresh material (preferably of the green variety, if available). This makes for quicker composting, for the materials are being acted upon whilst the heap is being built. There are no hard and fast rules about the amount of activator to use, but only a very small quantity is sufficient.

I find a clothes dampening sprinkler ideal for applying the liquid activator. This consists of a bottle with a small rosette sprinkler built into the cork, equally suitable for damping clothes or sprinkling small amounts of activator on the compost heap. The only snag is that, invariably, when the lady of the house is about to damp down the washing, the sprinkler bottle is in the garden shed. Shake the bottle before applying the activator. When building compost heaps, the writer has found the Quick Return compost activator easy to use, very successful and most fascinating. The horizontal method is recommended because few people have the time or opportunity to gather herbs. Also, as stated, the ready-made powder produces two tons of compost for only 1s. 9d.

The vertical way: For the benefit of those persons who do prefer to gather their own herbs we will take a look at the best way of using them. After first building the heap, holes about 1 foot apart are drilled with a crowbar, to a depth of about 6 inches from the bottom, throughout the heap. Then about 3 oz. of the liquid solution is poured into each hole, which is filled in tightly with dry soil. The heap is then covered and left for at least one month or more, depending upon the time of the year.

I have known gardeners who have gathered all the necessary herbs and, after preparation, made their own powder with successful results.

A Hive of Activity

To understand something about the way organic matter disintegrates makes for successful results. Let us assume you have carefully carried out the instructions regarding the construction of the container and site. The receptacle has now been filled with vegetable waste, weeds, grass cuttings and all the other suitable materials. Every type of heap quickly becomes a hive of activity. In the early stages, as the contents start to break down, quite a lot of heat is generated. Later, as juices are released, it cools down till it is just warm. It then becomes a breeding ground for millions of uncountable workers, as numerous as the grains of sand on a beach. Small insects, fungi, bacteria, and microscopic species all appear, live, die off, and like the multitudes before them, add their tiny bodies to the mass of humus being produced. Worms and larger insects appear, and each and every one plays a part, however small, in creating the compost heap. The earthworm has pride of place, and is the most vital worker. This massive army working like ants require air, so proper ventilation is essential. Equally with the worm, the activator plays a major role. The heap must not be allowed to become too wet or to dry out. All this paves the way for good, rich, friable compost, replete with all the ingredients of plant life. A sacking cover, or some other material which allows the heap to breathe, must be used to cover the top. This is most important to conserve the warmth. So the heap comes to life and like all living things it needs air and heat. It is most important to keep the top covered with sacking, or other material, which will not only retain the warmth but allow the heap to breathe.

Farms

When the Q.R. activator is employed on large estates, or for making farm compost, a dessertspoonful of the powder is put into a gallon of rain water. After being allowed to stand for twenty-four hours it is stirred well and may then be applied direct to the heap through a rose in a watering can.

Drainage and Rain

If the compost bin is on a light soil there is no problem

about drainage. With a heavy soil dig down for a depth of about 6 inches and put in some rubble, which should be covered with soil. Some heaps, especially those that contain a large amount of green substance, give off a lot of moisture. This should be allowed to drain off to avoid contents becoming too wet. For the same reason it is important to keep heavy rain off the heap; so a location under the branches of a small tree or bush is good. Excessive rain may cause the heap to lose heat or even putrify. If a heap has to be exposed during heavy rain, a sheet of corrugated iron or some other substance can be suspended over the sacking, not actually resting on the compost, but supported on the sides of the box. This will enable excess water to drain off.

Prevention of Smells

It is very unfortunate that many people are reluctant to even attempt building a compost heap because they think decaying vegetation gives off an offensive smell. However, you may be certain that if the methods described in this booklet are adopted there will be no smell. On the contrary there will be an aroma of sweet smelling compost, in four to eight weeks (according to the season). This will be like the leafmould in a forest.

It is important, however, to refrain from putting meat, fish, left-over cat or dog food in the heap. All these substances will attract flies, mice, and will certainly cause smells.

Charcoal

If a reader is still not happy about taking up composting because of undesirable smells, then the following simple remedy will prove one hundred per cent effective. Use a good supply of charcoal and spread it thickly over the soil where the heap is being built. Charcoal is the finest time proved agent for taking up all forms of odorous gases. In order to obtain a good supply of charcoal, simply make up a fire using old brushwood. Allow it to burn up rapidly till red hot throughout, when water should be poured over it. What remains will be your charcoal.

Weeds

For many years, in common with most other gardeners, I

carefully burnt all weeds, especially perennials. Since the great value of them to the compost heap has been revealed, all my weeds now find a place in compost, including those actually in seed and rampant ones. It is desirable to place them in the centre of the heap; even the notorious bindweed, dandelion roots, and diseased vegetables can all be successfully composted. The only growing things that cannot be composted are evergreens, holly, ivy and yew. Anything really tough, such as cabbage stalks, should be cut up into 6 inch pieces with a spade to aid decomposition.

Artificial Fertilizers versus Compost

From the time the first primitive man planted a few seeds, the entire world firmly believed in manures, humus, and the organic gardening and farming of the compost heap. A German, Von Liebig, shattered this time proved theory overnight when he wrote his remarkable book, *Chemistry of Agriculture and Physiology*. From 1840 onwards farming and gardening circles everywhere began to accept the artificial fertilizer. We cannot blame them, for Von Liebig, born 1803, was a brilliant scholar, with many chemical discoveries to his credit, the greatest being the fertilizer. Briefly, his theory was, why go to all the trouble of building compost heaps when the necessary chemicals, mainly nitrogen, phosphorous, and potash, can be produced in the laboratory? Even today, in spite of world-wide evidence that artificial fertilizers and insecticides abuse the soil, many still accept Liebig's theory.

It must be remembered that Liebig was a chemist and knew nothing about organic husbandry. However, learned men such as the late Sir Albert Howard, with a lifetime of experience in organic farming, rejected the chemical fertilizer. They considered chemicals could not compare with natural organic compost, and would prove dangerous if used for decades on a large scale. We now know conclusively, from the slow conversion of fertile farmland into deserts, just how true the humus theory of compost and organic farming really is; in spite of this, many stubbornly follow the theory of chemical fertilizers advocated by Von Liebig.

CHAPTER TWO

THE EARTHWORM

ALTHOUGH IT HAS taken a long time to prove, and many persons still have doubts, the earthworm plays a vital role in compost making. This little creature is the mainstay of all successful heaps. Darwin, in his theory of the species, tried to prove that the weight of the cattle which could be fed on any given pasture land was in direct relation to the number of worms contained within. There is a great deal of truth in this belief. Chemical fertilizer manufacturers will not agree, and may try to convince you that their products will beat the earthworm. Fortunately, many experienced farmers, nurserymen, market gardeners and thousands of garden owners accept the little worm as being essential to fertile soil and organic life. This theory is also endorsed by specialists who have studied the question of compost making and organic gardening for many decades. They are supported by agricultural experts, scientists, and other learned men.

An interesting report appeared in an August, 1969, issue of the *Daily Sketch* headed: 'Worm's Eye View of Hunger'. It went on to tell about a grammar schoolmaster who, in order to write a thesis for his B.A. Degree, collected 6,231 worms. A Government Department became deeply interested in this study of the simple little worm. In 1969 we went back to the theory of Darwin for the National Agriculture Service believes that the schoolmaster, a Mr. Pickering, may have solved the grave problem of getting sufficient food for hungry ponies. The work carried out by this teacher showed that in fertile parts of the New Forest there are some forty-two worms to every square yard. An official of the National Agriculture Service stated, 'Worms are a measure of soil fertility. Where the worms are the ground is good and animals have plenty to eat'. It is nearly ninety years since Charles Darwin, in his book, *Vegetable Mould and Earthworms*, forecast that without the earthworm, vegetation would gradually disappear likewise. He was ignored by many. Today, after a century of chemical farming, the 'Dust Bowls' of America and other countries show the truth of Darwin's statement.

Danger of Insecticides

Having shown how vital the worm is to successful organic gardening, let us take a look at a chemical pesticide and see how it acts in removing these little creatures from our beautiful lawns. After mixing, the solution is sprinkled over the grass and by morning the surface of the lawn is littered with the dead bodies of worms. The gardener's best friends are thus ruthlessly destroyed to bring beauty to the lawn by preventing worm casts. The organic gardener is perfectly happy to see worm casts—the richest humus on earth—he will put it to good use to feed crops and flowers. There is not another creature that plays such a vital role in our lives and in the history of the world as the earthworm. For generations writers have praised the worm and the way in which it has carried out a gigantic programme of work for man. Before the birth of Christ the Egyptians knew the value and secret of the earthworm. The Nile Delta possessed some of the richest soils in the world; its organic matter teemed with worms.

The practice of soaking the soil with unadulterated liquid horse manure can well prove fatal to worms. It has the effect of forcing a large number of them to the surface where they can easily be killed by sunshine.

So worms are more important today then ever before for soil fertility. This is especially true at a time when horse manure is almost impossible to obtain in sufficient quantities, and even when available, the cost to many is prohibitive. For this reason alone it is imperative to insure that an ever increasing number of worms exist in our soils.

From Fertile Land to Desert

The entire world's food supply is very much dependent on the worm, which tirelessly goes on cultivating the soil year after year. If the entire worm population of the world perished, the soil would gradually become one vast desert; all farmland would eventually become barren without the humus provided by our multitude of worms. Everything comes from the earth, and is, in one form or another, returned; decaying bodies, vegetation and so on. The worm exists on everything organic, which it in turn excretes as vital, living soil in the form of casts. Like pigs on land and crabs in the sea, earthworms are scavengers of the soils, making food out of everything that has lived and died, the remains of animals and other organisms, some so minute that they cannot be seen with the naked eye. As you may have observed, worms will pull leaves and other vegetable matter beneath the soil. Some earth and particles of sand are used by the worm to grind up this vegetable and animal matter.

Worm Casts

The worm's glandular secretions and nitrogen are mixed with the food in the process of eating. The end result consists of very fine worm casts rich in lime, minerals and vegetable matter. These casts contain glandular fluids from the body of the worm; these being essential for the growth of healthy plants and supplying everlasting humus to the soil, providing the cycle is allowed to continue. The casts are made of the finest particles which can be obtained and have the appearance of having been put through a fine sieve. Man cannot by any means produce such a wonderful organic fertilizer as these worm casts which are brought about by a natural process, an act of God. The average worm eats its own weight every day and therefore will daily excrete its own weight in humus.

Worm Casts and Soil

An interesting insight into the value of worm casts is shown when we compare them with soil.

Worm casts contain 7 times more nitrogen than soil

6	,,	,,	magnesium	,,	,,
3	,,	,,	potash	,,	,,
2	,,	,,	phosphorus	,,	,,
2	,,	,,	lime	,,	,,

Worms are known to exist mainly beneath the earth for periods up to about fourteen years. The worm will reproduce itself hundreds of times each year, which is wonderful for the organic gardener or farmer. In good organic soils rich in humus, hundreds of thousands of worms provide up to ten tons of worm casts each year per acre. They not only produce these casts, but do extensive tunnelling, allowing rain and air to penetrate the soil. There is a saying, 'breeding like rabbits', but worms excel this. Under ideal conditions, one thousand of them will produce forty million in two years. A good aim for the creation of ideal garden and farmland is to produce one million worms per acre. These will prove to be good and faithful servants, returning to each acre some two hundred tons of digested soil each year.

Lime

It is important to ensure that the vegetable plot or garden has sufficient lime. This enables the worm to work even better as a compost maker. To ensure lime content is right, a soil test should be carried out, for it is equally important not to add excessive amounts of lime merely on guesswork.

Let the Worm do your digging

It is less laborious and more economical to let the worm do your digging. The results, which have to be seen to be believed, are far superior to those obtained by back aching digging. When a garden is dug, the results of months of labour by the worm is ruined. Digging has become a habit, but a bad one, as every organic gardener will prove from his own results. With every plot of land goes a spade. Gardeners enthusiastically set about winter digging and double digging, advocated by all the gardening books and magazines. Old habits and customs die hard. The contention that digging makes for drainage plus aeration of the soil, and is essential, is not upheld if you examine an organically composted, unturned plot, rich in humus. The multitude of worms here are busy doing the digging every minute of the day, year in and year out. Unfortunately most gardeners follow the advice of the experts and carry out their digging religiously. So did I for more years than I care to remember—but never again. One of the main reasons put forward for such extensive digging is to allow a greater surface of the soil to be exposed to frost and snow. There is no difference in the effects of the elements on a soil that has been dug than on a soil left undug. The frost will still lift up the firm ground all over and it will get the benefits. The theory of the experts sounds convincing and has been handed down from father to son since man first cultivated the land. It is very debatable, for what they gain by doing this (if anything), is lost through the damage done to worm life by destroying many burrows which the worms have to construct all over again. The secret and great advantage of the no-digging system is that the earthworm is left to keep open the lower layers of soil, whereas the frost deals with the top. So all the advantages are obtained without labour and there is no need to break up the soil for planting—also it remains level. The worm does not get such complaints as hernia, but you might! The digestive juices of the earthworm do aid plants and crops in deriving necessary vital substances from the soil.

The Worm Farm's system of introducing worms into poor type soils proved to be successful in enriching the land. First, the earth needing the treatment is tested and the P.H. value corrected with the addition of lime. There are then two simple methods of increasing the worm population (1) By spreading worm-rich compost at intervals on the land (2) By the introduction of baby worms or capsules into the compost heaps. Once you have got an adequate worm population you may say with confidence, 'Let the worm do my digging'.

So our soil is really alive—if we allow it to live. Each spadeful will present a miracle of organic activity and the soil becomes a battleground of every species living off one another and in so doing keeping a balance, which is the natural state of affairs. When this delicate balance has been disturbed by man over a long period by the introduction of poisons, no one can forecast with any certainty what the results will be in the years ahead.

A Farm with Millions of Livestock

England has been an agricultural country for centuries.

However, since the great Industrial Revolution, valuable farmland has been gradually swallowed up by the expansion of towns and, more recently, motor roads. In spite of this, one particular farm is really progressing; the Cumberland Worm Farm. It is perhaps little known to the average person, but in fact holds a record of having over 50 million head of livestock. This is not a fairy story but fact. The farm has more animals in the form of juicy worms than all the other farms put together. Between them, these masses of worms produce tons of the finest organic fertilizer known to man anywhere in the wide world. Starting in a comparatively small way to meet the need of anglers throughout the country, this farm complex has developed a flourishing business in providing for:

Agriculture and Horticulture. Landscaping. Land Reclamation. Fishing. Mole Catching. Giving advice and assistance to organizations such as the Land Reclamation Department and the Electricity Board on the treatment of derelict slag heaps.

The most important use to which these worms are being put —as this booklet will show—is agriculture. Started on a 2 acre site at Kirklinton, Carlisle, Cumberland in 1965, the Cumberland Worms Farms Ltd, have made rapid progress. A lady became the first manager and in 1967 over four million worms were sold. Employed at the farm at first were fourteen ladies, for no kind of mechanical machines can take the place of skilled fingers in counting and sorting the endless number of worms. Perhaps not the job that our girl friends would relish. A skilled 'farm labourer' is able to count over one thousand of these little compost makers per hour. Worms are sold at a fair price which compares more than favourably with horse manure, when you can get it. The farm has made tremendous progress, rapid expansion, and sends worms to many overseas countries.

Rapid Multiplication

Masses of worms are reared in boxes under cover and outside, in specially prepared beds, to prevent their escape. Wonderful livestock which will increase yields for all are produced in this way. The future of these worms means great progress in the business of soil fertilization.

Worm Capsules

A problem encountered in the farming and sale of worms is that it is difficult to change the environment of an adult earthworm. They do not take very kindly to being literally uprooted and transplanted in the soil of some far-off farm or garden. This is overcome by introducing worms into a compost heap by means of capsules, each containing up to four worms or baby worms. By using this method, the worms survive after appearing from the capsule in a compost heap on foreign land.

Many Species

There are some thirty-five different varieties of the earthworm in England. Special strains are bred to get best results from the task of converting organic waste into wonderful compost. This is necessary for treatment of areas where the soil has been devitalized by incorrect farming methods—the earthworm producing its everlasting humus in the form of casts. It has been estimated that worms in England produce no less than 10 million tons of humus each year.

Worm Breeding

About six hundred worms may be bred in 1 cu. ft. of soil. This is by no means as complicated a problem as one might think. One requires a wooden box with no openings. Fill almost to the top with soil containing a good supply of organic matter. The box should be kept in an even temperature with the soil moist. A mature worm will produce a capsule about every ten days, each capsule containing a number of young worms. It is a profitable business when we remember that each worm comprises both male and female sex organs and, after mating, both can produce capsules. Within about six to twelve months sufficient worms will be produced to impregnate two large compost heaps.

Separating Worms and Capsules

It is not easy to search for the worms or capsules. Use a sheltered warm corner and tip the contents of the box on top of some dry material, such as cardboard, into a conical heap and leave it for about one hour. During this time the worms will proceed into the centre to get away from the cool air and light. The capsules remain, so by removing the outer layers of the soil one obtains a large percentage of them which may be utilized to start other compost heaps or to stock breeding boxes. The worm does not always relish a change of location, or organic feeding substances, so needs time to get used to a new site. If a fair amount of soil or compost is transferred with the worms, this condition makes for better breeding. Having removed the outer layers of soil from the conical heap with the bulk of the capsules, what remains at the centre contains the worms which can be used for further breeding. This collecting of capsules may be carried out every four weeks or, in exceptionally hot weather, at shorter intervals.

Miraculous Compost Maker

Having taken a brief look at the life and habits of the earthworm, we see it has characteristics not found in any other creature. It is a vital part of organic gardening. Soil lacking a good supply of worms is short of humus, for each and every one of these tiny worms is a 'living compost maker'.

CHAPTER THREE

MANY SYSTEMS OF ORGANIC GARDENING

THOSE ENGAGED IN organic cultivation can adopt various ways to achieve the same results. Let us once again consider the question of digging. If you have taken over a garden, or plot of land, that has been neglected for years and become overgrown like a jungle, then you are compelled to resort to digging. An excellent way to clear such weed infested soil is to plant a crop of potatoes, digging up many perennial weeds in the process. This certainly helps to clear the land, for when the potatoes are lifted any remaining perennial weeds can be likewise removed. Such neglected plots are very likely to be a breeding ground for wireworms which do extensive damage to potatoes, so traps need to be set for these. An effective trap is to put a potato on a stick a few inches into the soil. On taking it out after a few days it will be found to be teeming with wireworms.

Breaking up weed infested, overgrown land is the only case where I would advocate digging. On other soils the important question concerns the length of time the organic system has been employed. What is vital, and the deciding factor in the change over from dug to undug plots, is the amount of organic compost available. On any vegetable plot a 'no digging' programme can be introduced providing an abundant supply of organic compost is used and spread over the entire surface of the soil to a depth of one inch in the autumn.

All vegetable growers who cultivate root crops such as potatoes, carrots, Jerusalem artichokes, parsnips and so on, are compelled to dig when lifting the vegetables. As crops are rotated every third year, the entire plot is subjected to this form of digging once in three years. This likewise applies to the flower garden when such flowers as gladioli and dahlias are dug up in the autumn. However, the planting of such vegetable seeds and tubers or flower corms on good organic soil can be carried out without digging, by simply using a dibber.

Composting—various ways

(1) *Rudolf Steiner's* bio-dynamic system, a time proved method of obtaining supplies of organic compost, named after the devoted man who perfected it. Unfortunately it is rather too involved for the gardener and small holder. The heaps need turning, so a farm or large estate is more suitable for adaptation to this system.

(2) *The Indore Method.* Sir Albert Howard, who farmed at Indore, India, from 1910 to 1923, became an expert in composting. His method, famous the world over, took the name of the place where he farmed. Like the Steiner system it is most suited to farmland, or estates with livestock and labour. Rudolf Steiner and Sir Albert can be regarded as pioneers who paved the way everywhere for organic gardeners. Many organic gardening systems are based on one of these two methods.

(3) *Quick Return Compost.* This way of composting has been proved by the writer in his organic garden for a long time. It is simple to introduce and equally excellent for the small gardener or farmer with thousands of acres. The amount of labour involved is negligible, and the entire procedure is interesting and fascinating. Discovered by Miss Bruce after years of trial and error, it is quick in every sense of the word. No turning of heaps is required and compost can be made by anyone; even an elderly person, providing the interest is at heart and the gardener wants the best from a living soil.

History of Quick Return Compost

This method of Quick Return compost making has brought organic gardening within the reach of every gardener. It was, to quote Miss Bruce's own words, 'about 1925' that she first heard of Dr. Steiner's method of composting, and as a result joined the Anthroposophical Agricultural Foundation. From this body – the English branch of Steiner's bio-dynamic movement – Miss Bruce became acquainted with compost making for the first time in her life. Becoming very deeply interested in the subject, she visited Holland and saw the bio-dynamic farms and observed the manner in which they were organized. Her feelings were that, good as Rudolf Steiner's method was, there must be a less complicated system to meet the needs of all interested in the land, from the household gardener to the owners of large farms or estates. With this object in view she commenced to carry out a long series of experiments. It was a book about herbs, entitled *Nature's Remedies*, that finally gave this painstaking lady the clue she sought. She learned that certain plants, between them, contained all the elements of vegetative life. For example, yarrow and stinging nettle made a perfect combination of plant life essentials. Yarrow contains iron, lime, soda, potash, phosphorus, sulphur, and nitrates. Stinging nettle, on the other hand, has oil, formic acid, ammonia, carbonic acid and iron. Miss Bruce continued to experiment with these and other plants which had vital elements.

Final Success

She finally extracted the juice from the living plants of yarrow, nettle, dandelion, chamomile and valerian. To these she added an infusion of oak bark. She then filled a number of jars with chopped up vegetable substances, lawn mowings, weeds, nettles, and so on. Each jar was then subjected to treatment by mixing a solution of the liquid obtained from the living plants in the ratios as shown: 1 : 10, 1 : 30, 1 : 60, 1 : 100 and, on a sudden impulse, she decided on a fourth solution of 1 : 10,000. The jars were labelled and the labels turned to the wall. Even after only five days it was noted that the contents of one jar had changed colour rapidly. In fifteen days it became apparent that one jar was best, in fact almost broken down to compost. The first one to break down was the 1 : 10,000, second 1 : 100, third 1 : 60, and so on.

Comparison of two Systems

Miss Bruce constructed two compost heaps, one treated by the Rudolf Steiner method and the other by Q.R. Compost in ratio of 1 : 10,000 parts. When these heaps had become compost, a well-known soil analyst examined the contents of both and his findings were, 'of equal manurial value'.

When compost heaps are mentioned the word does not mean 'heap' in the literal sense, for all compost layers are built as level as possible.

Alwyn Seifert A German, Herr Alwyn Seifert, like many other experts, has devoted his life to organic farming. He wrote a book entitled *Compost*, which became a best seller and was translated into English. In the main, Seifert's theory is similar to the other systems of composting. Boxes are not used, but a shallow trench is dug out and the heap built up with the sides sloping inwards like a potato clamp. Again, this system of compost making is more suitable for farms, with labour and livestock, for heaps require turning. After every 6 inch layer has been built, lime is sprinkled on at the rate of 1 lb. per cubic yard of compost. It is quite a problem, for after the heap is completed it is soaked in liquid manure. After being built in the autumn it is left to the spring and then turned.

I tried the system of Seifert for many years (before reading his book), but used a compost box. It is successful but takes a long time and cannot be compared with the efficient Q.R. method. Alwyn Seifert, in common with all experts in this field, maintains that every vegetable or weed may be placed on the heap, whether diseased or not. The disease spores, black fly, weed seeds or roots are all killed off in the intense heat built up in the heap.

Seifert considered that good black organic soil contained what he termed 'lasting humus' or humic acids combined with secretions from the digestive system of tiny creatures. This humus could not be added to land by any other means, nor could it be washed or carried away, once the cycle had been allowed to develop over the years. He also thinks that every weed plays an important role in overcoming deficiencies in the soil. This is understandable when it is realized that Miss Bruce found two notorious weeds, nettle and dandelion, to contain practically all the elements of plant life.

Other Organic Activators

There are a number of equally good organic activators including:

Alginure compost activator, which is a seaweed jelly made up in 1 lb. tins. Fertosan activator, a bacterial culture in powder form. Marinure seaweed activator, which is also a combined organic fertilizer. All three of these activators can be obtained from The Henry Doubleday Research Association.

The Bio-Dynamic Approach

Bio-Dynamic farming and gardening in no way differs from the established practices of sound organic husbandry; but it seeks to supplement them in various ways because it appears that the earth by itself is no longer able to provide the nourishment required for the full development of the whole man—body, soul, and spirit. From the B-D point of view, when we take a crop off the land we remove not only substances but also forces, and the latter are, if anything, more important than the former. Orthodox agriculture aims to replace the lost substance and even to build it up, by means of materials taken from the cheapest possible source in the mineral realm: as a result the force reservoir in the soil is depleted and the produce, though bulky, is often diseased, contaminated and lacking in the qualities needed even for bodily health.

Organic farmers recognize the need to maintain a thriving soil population of micro-organisms, and keep as far as possible to erstwhile living material in their methods of manuring. B-D goes one step further and seeks consciously to build up the force reservoir both in soil and manure by means of various sprays and preparations in small quantities, such as are used in homoeopathy. The aim is to create a sensitive harmony between the soil and growing plants.

Plants and the Soil

The relationship between plant and soil is seen to be so intimate that, even physically, it is often difficult to define where the roots end and where the soil begins. Together they form an interconnected web through which one species of plant can influence others at quite appreciable distances; some of these mutual influences are sympathetic and beneficial, others are adverse. This complex web can be seen in a still wider perspective, and the whole plant/soil cover of the globe then appears as a sense organ of the organism Earth, through which it is able to perceive and react to its cosmic environment.

Modern science is probing more and more deeply into the minute mechanisms of life and into the vast mechanisms of the universe. These efforts are meeting with some success and must be given their due respect. But since they are based on a materialistic outlook and neglect the inter-relatedness of the whole cosmos, they must lead to a one-sided and unco-ordinated control over the life of the planet which could well end in catastrophe. For real success a different approach and a deeper understanding are necessary.

Proof that the No-Digging System Really Works

It is no easy task to persuade gardeners, young or old, that the spade can become a tool for limited use, they are almost without exception so conditioned to digging. Instead of doing my winter digging this autumn, I am in the process of writing this little booklet, which I hope may convince you that deep digging is not only a waste of energy, but in the long run does more harm than good. At this time of the year thousands of gardeners and allotment holders do their rough digging before winter sets in and the ground becomes frozen. Mine is being carried out by a multitude of worms below a covering of or-ganic compost. Old habits and customs die hard. Anyone taking up gardening for the first time looks around to see what his neighbours are doing. Following this ancient traditional cus-tom, practically everywhere digging is being carried out, so that the newcomer likewise becomes a slave to the spade. Almost all books and magazines on the subject advocate digging. Well, is digging really necessary? Do you want ample proof that it is not?

Arkley Manor Gardens

A well-known organic gardener, Dr. W. E. Shewell-Cooper, has proved conclusively for many years at his organic gardens at Arkley Manor, that we may dispense with digging. This gentleman's slogan is: 'At Arkley Manor—No Digging—No Forking—No Hoeing'. The proof of this system lies in the fact that for years abundant fruit and vegetable crops and beautiful flowers have been grown; no chemical fertilizers or harmful insecticides are used. The system adopted by Dr. Shewell-Cooper is simply organic gardening. Once again we see the elements of a natural garden being brought into play. The entire surface of the soil is covered with compost known as mulching for just one inch in depth. If you do not have sufficient compost, then Dr. Shewell-Cooper recommends the use of sedge peat, which is equally suitable for preventing the growth of annual weeds. This is far more effective than hoeing, without doing the damage hoeing always causes. Forking, digging and hoeing bring an ever increasing number of weed seeds to the surface, where, because conditions are ideal, they germinate. Without being brought to the surface such seeds would have remained dormant for years.

Pest Control

This, whenever possible at Arkley Manor, is carried out by natural means. No poison sprays are used. When necessary, only Pyrethrum or Derris are used; the latter comes from powdered roots of the Derris bush. It kills insects but does no harm to animals or humans. Every flower bed is given a mulch of compost or medium grade sedge peat to a depth of one inch. The only attention for years is simply to add a little more of the peat. An abundant supply of compost is obtained by the use of four large wooden bins containing four tons of compost each. These are being filled up all the while with all types of garden waste, including old newspapers, which are torn and damped first. As soon as the last bin has been filled the first is ready for emptying. This compost is applied direct to the soil at the rate of two bucketfuls per square yard. For an activator, fish manure is used, this is applied at the rate of three oz. per square yard for every depth of six inch layer of organic matter collected and placed in the bins.

Does Dr. Shewell-Cooper's garden at Arkley Manor prove that organic gardening, with little or no digging, really works?

Well, Open Days are held so you can go along and see for yourself. It is interesting to note that there are 7½ acres of land and the whole has been cultivated by these mini-work-methods for ten years with a minimum of labour—only three men being employed. I think you must agree that all this speaks very well for the system used and supports the belief that organic gardening really produces best results.

The Good Gardeners Association

Founded on a national basis to help all gardeners, subscriptions being £2 each year for Fellows, £1 for old age pensioners and students of agriculture. Dr. Shewell-Cooper edits a monthly news letter for the Association giving an up-to-date account of gardening events which is sent free to members.

A well-known soils expert will carry out soil analysis free for all Fellows.

CHAPTER FOUR

METHODS OF CONTROLLING INSECTS

INSECTS MAY NOT be regarded as being a vital species of life in the world, until we consider they comprise at least four-fifths of all animals on the earth. Some experts place the ratio of insects to other species as high as 5 : 6. The study of insects, entomology, is a most fascinating subject, and one soon begins to realize that they are of great importance to man, both medically and economically, and comprise the main food of many other creatures. Many interesting books have been written on this subject with varying estimates of the number of varieties. Some experts place the figure at about a million, while others settle for a more conservative 600,000 or more species of these little creatures. Whichever figure we accept, the fact remains that the insect population of the world is formidable, especially as many thousands of new insects are discovered and classified every year. This brings greater interest to one of the least understood sciences, for knowledge of the insect world is changing continuously and to remain an expert on entomology one must keep up to date with recent discoveries. To illustrate what a vast subject this is, counts have been made in the Italian Alps of more than one million nests of red ants housing some three hundred billion ants. It has been estimated that in the course of a year these ants could destroy up to 15,000 tons of other insect pests. From our glimpse into this world of insects it will be shown how this mighty force plays a vital role in our lives. Insects cannot be separated from plants, animals or other forms of life, for whatever happens in the insect world can effect us all in one way or another. If the estimated number of red ants sounds exaggerated, let us compare the results when nature runs wild in creating swarms of locusts. A massive swarm of these creatures can be so dense that they blacken the sky like a massive sand storm and, in passing, cut out some of the sunshine. Locusts settling on a crop of grain can completely devour it in less than twenty minutes. There is such a horde of these hungry creatures that a large number of them can attack every growing part of the crop. DDT and other insecticides have played an important role in the past by destroying plagues of insects, thereby saving crops and preventing starvation. In such isolated cases the insecticide has often been sprayed from aircraft.

In every garden, under normal conditions, a balance exists among insects which is controlled by food, parasites, disease, predators and weather conditions. Many pests do not survive a severe winter. Regarding pests, and the insects and birds that prey on them, a state of war exists all the time. For all manner of reasons in the past this balance changed continuously and for centuries man could do little to control it. However, since the advent of insecticides, weed killers and herbicides, man is ruthlessly able to exert a devastating influence over these forces.

All Species Perish

Apart from other considerations, the chemical insecticide has yet to be discovered which will kill only the pest and cause no other harm. Our study of the compost heap showed that all insects played a role in aiding the gardener, even if only in casting their minute bodies to form humus. One expert in England estimated that there are 625,000 different species of insects and hundreds more are added to the list every year. The vast majority aid the gardener in one way or another. So over the years, plagues of unwanted species permitting, it is vital to allow the bulk of these tiny creatures to live.

Organic gardeners have to contend with pests just as everyone does who plants crops and flowers. However, a far better balance exists in an organic garden, where, as often as possible, every creature is allowed to play its proper role, and a composted soil rich in humus, and alive with worms, makes for healthy disease-resisting plants. If a particular species of pest such as blackfly gets out of hand, certain safe methods of control can be employed. These are given in detail in Chapter Six.

War on Insects

We must accept the fact that some species of insects devour crops and flowers and this must be prevented. Blackfly, greenfly, plant lice, and a host of others, if left unchecked, will ruin a vegetable plot and flower beds. Gardeners using insecticide sprays and powders think it is a simple matter to eliminate such pests. This is true for months or even years, but gradually, slowly but surely, insects build up resistance to the insecticides. Nature's way of protection results in thousands of eggs being laid and eventually some survive the onslaught of the insecticide. From such eggs, few as they may be, a strain gradually develops which has this built-in resistance to the poison.

At Arnas in Sweden, house-flies became so immune to DDT that sprays over two hundred times stronger than a killer dose proved harmless. This will apply to any form of life if its fecundity is strong enough. A classical example of the ability of animals to survive a lethal poison can be seen in the case of rabbits slowly building up a resistance to myxomatosis.

The question of resistance is only one of the grave problems about insecticides. They are produced in such large numbers that sufficient investigation into the total effects on man, animal, insect and—last but far from least—the soil, is impossible.

Insecticides and Pollution bring Disaster

Years of indiscriminate use of insecticides have to be carefully studied to assess the total effects on both insects and soil. It is an extremely complicated issue, vast sums of money are involved, and an ever increasing number of chemicals are produced with insufficient study of the long term effects on all forms of wildlife. Experts are happy to give the all clear on an insecticide after an investigation into the short term effects only. Little interest is taken over what may happen in the next few decades, or the persistency of the poison in the soil. The B.B.C.'s outstanding film on the destruction of Loch

Leven presents a vivid but terrible picture of the long term effects of insecticides and pollution with total destruction of every form of life that, slowly but surely turned a beautiful lake into a polluted cesspool.

Do Insecticides Produce more Pests?

Having sprayed the crop on farm or garden with a powerful insecticide, we can be sure that it carries out its work swiftly and thoroughly. However, investigations reveal some rather peculiar and disturbing facts about insecticides and insects. The extermination of the swarm of pests is only the beginning of a chain of events, not the end. Researches show that in some instances our poison sprays aid the insect population by improving both metabolism and fertility. From a number of eggs of mites (*Doryphora*) it was found that these increased alarmingly when the female species were fed on potato leaves that had been dusted with a number of insecticides—providing some days elapsed between the application of the powder and the time of eating, to let the poison disappear. So the potatoes, after being treated with the insecticide, contained something which not only brings no harm to the insects but aids their ability to breed.

Further Investigations

Further studies were made in an effort to determine:

(1) If toxic chemicals have any effects on plants.

(2) If so, whether this is good or bad for insects.

Observations over a long period indicated 'Yes' to question 1. The chemical industries will always maintain that chemicals are not harmful to plants, which increase in size and become greener after treatment.

Chemical fertilizers and insecticides do produce abundant crops. We can all see cauliflowers larger than footballs, carrots which are more like parsnips in size.

Vines which had been subjected to numerous insecticides and fungicides (these included DDT, parathion, sevin, and sulphur), were examined. The leaves were tested for amino acids, nitrogen, phosphorus, potassium, calcium and magnesium. It was revealed that five-sixths of the plants treated with DDT and four-sixths of those treated with the other chemicals contained higher than average amino acids. So it was established that these poisons change the equilibrium of plants.

The most remarkable thing is that the answer to question 2—based on experiments conducted by numerous investigators —is yes, insects do benefit from insecticides. There are ample published references to support this claim. On fruit and nut trees, outbreaks of mites often follow the application of DDT. The same happened with beans after using lindane and malathion, likewise on vines when phosphoric compounds have been employed. There are many and varied theories as to why certain insecticides, after their initial successful use, cause even greater numbers of mites in subsequent years. It is considered by some that the poison has ever greater effect on natural enemies of the mites. So with biological control curtailed, the mites breed more rapidly than ever.

The grave problem is that manufacturers of insecticides and all others concerned have not devoted sufficient time to study the long term effects on ecology. Insecticide experts have disregarded or completely ignored any other forms of control.

CHAPTER FIVE

BIOLOGICAL CONTROL OF INSECTS, PLANTS AND WEEDS

PRIOR TO CHEMICAL farming, biological control of insects was tried and in many places is still used successfully. It is believed that Erasmus Darwin, grandfather of Charles, was the first person to advocate biological control in his *Philosophy of Agriculture and Gardening* published in 1800. He considered aphids could well be destroyed by the breeding of the larvae of hoverflies—experts in this field have since proved how right he was. Biological control simply means reducing pests by the use of natural agencies such as parasites, predators, diseases or even other plants. This method of control has been known for a long time. The insects used for these purposes have sometimes been brought from another country, or reared in specially designed factories, or occasionally they already exist in another part of the country. In some cases this system of control has met with spectacular, almost unbelievable success, but in other instances it has been a miserable failure. An outstanding example of nature allowing massive biological control is seen in the Italian Alps, where the red ants from over one million nests are estimated to destroy as much as 15,000 tons of pest insects in one year. In the U.S.A. they have made far greater use of biological control than in England. For a long time in history only natural control was needed, but much has happened in the last hundred years to disturb nature.

Use of Ladybirds

This brief introduction to the role played by ladybirds in aiding man shows what wonderful results can be accomplished. These pretty little creatures prove to be one of our greatest assets. After laying masses of eggs, mostly on leaves, hatching takes place within a few days; the young make gluttons of themselves in devouring batches of every type of crop and flower destroying aphids. A stream or even a small fish pool greatly helps in aiding ladybirds to breed.

Biological control—U.S.A.

The Americans have developed ladybird breeding into a fine art. Many species are sent by post to aid farmers and gardeners alike. Our little ladybird has a long history of success, for it was used effectively in California in 1910. The orchards were then being ruined by plant bugs, so large numbers of ladybirds were taken from the mountains to the orchards. They attacked all the pests and the orchards were saved. Unfortunately, after this insecticides were used, until during World War II there was a shortage of chemicals and the ladybird again became famous. In 1943 a firm in California sent colonies of ladybirds to farmers all over the U.S.A. Over 50,000 ladybirds were used for one orchard.

Ladybirds from Australia

At one time the entire Californian fruit crop was imperilled by a massive invasion of scale insects. No local insects were able to combat them. Entomologists considered that the Australian ladybird *Cryptoleaemus Montrouzieri* would prove the answer to biological control. To adopt this control, ladybird factories were built at Riverside, California, and in Spain. It was estimated that in 1928, forty-eight million ladybirds were despatched from the Riverside factory to the citrus plantations. The results were truly astounding, the ladybirds proving more than a match for scale insects. Finally, a species of ladybird was reared which adapted itself to the climate of California and thrived; this did away with the necessity of building ladybird factories.

Some Insects from Foreign Parts bring Disaster

In America it is believed that the bulk of insect pests were taken into the country. An outstanding example of this took place in 1870 when the devastating cottony-cushion scale reached California on some acacia trees from Australia. This insect does extensive damage to citrus trees, and, having no natural enemies in California, it played havoc throughout all the orchards. The situation became desperate for no insecticide could be found to control the pest and destruction of the citrus industry was in the balance. America sent an entomologist to Australia and his investigations showed that a number of insects, including a species of ladybirds, controlled the cottony-cushion scale by feeding on it. These particular kind of ladybirds were taken to California and bred there. On being released into the plantations they destroyed this persistent pest, crops were saved, and within one year everything was back to normal.

An important lesson was learnt; that if plant feeding insects remain in their natural environment, invariably enemies exist which reduce the number. A grave problem may arise when such insects are taken to another country, or place, where their enemies are non-existent. Under these conditions they are likely to multiply alarmingly and cause widespread damage, destroying entire crops.

Biological Control can be Superior to Using Insecticides

A most interesting comparison of biological and chemical control occurred in central California. By 1946 DDT had been used extensively on citrus crops, resulting in the almost total destruction of the remarkable little ladybird which controls the cottony-scale insect. So once again in this beautiful country the balance of nature was disturbed and the entire crop was again threatened. It was only after the effects of DDT had somewhat diminished that the ladybird could once again be established and so serve its lifelong natural purpose in devouring the cushiony-scale. These little insects did just this and once again the fruit growers of California were saved from disaster and the world reaped the benefits of luscious crops of citrus fruit.

Biological Control of Plants and Weeds

Many people are inclined to regard all insects as enemies.

Yet many species are of great value to man, since they can be used to control other pests. Most insects feed on plants and their importance to plant ecology remains to be explored. They keep a balance among plants by sucking sap, eating leaves, seeds, roots, and flowers. It is when insects are in massive numbers that the true picture of their miraculous power is shown. Apart from assessing the effect of insects as pollinators, entomologists have not devoted much study to their effect on vegetation. Insects are vital in keeping a balance of nature, as is shown when this is disrupted by taking plants or wild animals to another country. Australia became a rabbit's paradise, they had no natural enemies and multiplied beyond man's wildest dreams. An insect, the mosquito, was taken to Australia and it rapidly spread myxomatosis among the rabbits.

Insects can Work Miracles

A classic example of the amazing way in which insects will aid man occurred in Australia. Admiral Arthur Phillip became the first Governor of New South Wales. In 1887 this gentleman of the senior service took cochineal insects and prickly pear (cacti) plants, as food for them, to Australia from Brazil. His intention was to provide cochineal to dye service uniforms red. Most species of the prickly pear come from South and Central America and have been taken overseas as hedging plants, sometimes with unforseeably drastic results. Australian conditions proved ideal and the prickly pear spread rapidly. By 1925, sixty million acres of farmland and forests became a massive jungle. Admiral Phillip's misguided idea of smartening service uniforms proved successful in swallowing up one million acres of land every year. Australian entomologists observed the habits of the prickly pear in America. As a result, three billion eggs of the Argentine moth (*Cactoblastis Cactorum*) were released in Australia in 1930. Within seven years the massive jungle of prickly pear had been eliminated, every scrap being devoured by the hordes of hungry caterpillars developed from these moths. What is also equally hard to believe is that the cost of clearing sixty million acres of near jungle was one penny per acre. Previous unsuccessful attempts by using insecticides had cost £10 per acre. A remarkable achievement for natural methods over chemicals at a saving of £59,750,000 —assuming the sixty million acres had been cleared by chemicals at £10 per acre.

Success in Other Countries

The example quoted from Australia is one of the most outstanding cases in the world but there are many others. By 1902 in Hawaii, farm and grazing land had been overrun by a shrub, *Lantana Camara*. A scale insect was taken by chance to Hawaii and it proved a bitter enemy of the shrub. Finally, eight species of insect were introduced into Hawaii, including: seed flies, leaf miners, lace bugs, three species of moths and two of butterflies. These insects have resulted in this weed-like shrub being kept under control.

During the late nineteenth century extensive pasture land and plantations in Fiji were ruined by a shrub, *Clidemia Hirta*, or Koster's Curse. There were no local insects to combat this shrub. The same shrub grows in Trinidad but is kept under control. In 1930 entomologists, after investigations in Trinidad, introduced small thrips to Fiji and in less than two years the jungle of shrubs had been brought under control.

In Mauritius during 1948 the black sage was effectively dealt with by seed-eating wasps and leaf beetles.

Many of the world's pasture lands have been rendered useless by St. John's Wort or Klamath weed. Great success over this weed has been achieved in the U.S.A., Australia, and New Zealand. The main insect used for this control is a beetle, *Chrysolina Quadrigemina*.

Much has yet to be learnt about the use of insects to control weeds. Outstanding success has been gained in many countries. Rigid control, experiments, and care have prevented the insects being used from becoming pests themselves. There are obviously a lot more investigations to be made into biological control. It is attractive in being natural and economical; plants, soils, and wild life are safeguarded from side-effects of insecticides. Pests are unable to build up a resistance to this kind of control.

Insects and Diseases

Can insects be infected with disease as a means of control? To infect insects with virus diseases or bacteria always seems distasteful to me, and is a reminder of the highly secret experiments into chemical warfare. Admittedly, scientists tell us there is no danger to humans or animals, for diseases of insects are not the same as those of man, and vice versa.

CHAPTER SIX

ORGANIC INSECTICIDES AND OTHER NATURAL MEANS OF CONTROL

FOR CENTURIES PARASITES and predators kept a balance in the world of insects which has been disturbed by insecticides killing them indiscriminately. The perfect pesticide is yet to be discovered, so man must seek biological and other means of control. The manner in which parasites exert their influence is shown with the white cabbage butterfly. The majority of the caterpillars of this butterfly become victims of the tiny ichneumon fly, one of the finest of parasites, but there are thousands more in the insect world. Organic insecticides derived from plants, flowers and herbs can be used against all manner of pests and diseases.

Identification

It pays gardeners to learn to recognize insects, good and bad. Books and leaflets often provide coloured charts giving full details of various species. In America, of 86,000 species of insects, 76,000 were classified directly as being friends of the gardener or providing an advantage to the soil.

Biological Control in America

In the U.S.A., insect parasites brought from India and Pakistan deal effectively with olive scale, while ladybirds from Australia carry out most valuable control, as described in Chapter Five. Parasites from France combat elm and fig scale and the hornet is a great destroyer of cabbage worms. If pests gain a hold they must be destroyed by all the means available, using parasites, traps and as a last resort, organic sprays or powders. An easy and economical way of controlling pests is to encourage birds in your garden.

Disease Resisting Plants

Growers, in recent years have to a great extent been safe-guarded by many and varied plants and vegetables that have been produced with a special built-in resistance to disease. Such varieties of potatoes, seeds or plants are sold as being immune from such and such a disease. Another preventive measure is to obtain early varieties of plants or seeds which mature before the particular pest or disease becomes effective. Much more work has to be done in this field, but it seems, briefly, the reason plants are able to resist disease and pests is because of toxic materials in the plant cells.

Garlic

An ancient herb which has aided man in living free from disease for centuries will prevent borers from attacking peach trees. If cloves of garlic are planted around the trees, close to the trunks, the peach borer will not appear. Up to 20% extract of garlic powder prepared in the form of a spray will combat mildew and scab in cucumbers, bean rust and tomato blight. Professors Ark and James, University of California, found that garlic will kill off much bacteria that appears on fruit and nut trees and on vegetables.

Chives and Other Plants

If chives are planted between rose bushes and climbers, aphids will be deterred. Try this simple remedy and see for yourself how successful it will prove. Chives make a useful addition to salads and soups; clumps should be split up and separated every third year. Likewise, tomatoes planted near an asparagus bed will ward off the asparagus beetle. Horse radish will prevent the potato bug and green beans will deter the Colorado beetle. Other herbs are also useful in aiding the gardener in insect control. Tansy deters ants. Anise and coriander contain oils which can be used in spray form to kill spider mites and aphids. Various flowers likewise have repellant properties, these include marigolds, asters, and chrysanthemums. It must be borne in mind, however, that the more fertile your soil, the less insect damage, and in the same proportion that fertility and humus decreases, so insect pests flourish.

Entomologists have produced insect attractors and repellants; perfumes are also used and lights for moths and insect traps. A problem with traps is that friendly insects also become victims.

Organic Pesticides

Derris and pyrethrum in powder or spray form are the most effective for organic gardeners. The latter is derived from a flower especially cultivated in Kenya for insect control. Derris is obtained from powdered roots of the derris bush and is much stronger and more effective, killing a large number of pests. Both these insecticides are safe for humans and animals alike, but should only be used as a last resort and not indiscriminately. They should only be applied after sundown when bees, wasps and other valuable insects have finished their useful work.

Extensive tests with ammonium sulphamate or amcide prove it to be both very effective and safe as a weed killer. It will destroy thistles, nettles, convolvulus, couch grass and brambles. A plastic can is advisable because amcide will corrode iron. Unlike chemicals employed for the same purpose, amcide is safe and thoroughly reliable.

Dormant oil sprays are very effective to combat scale insects, mites, red spider, aphids, thrips and mealybugs. A 3% mixture of the oil should be sprayed on fruit trees before the buds open. It must always be borne in mind that even organic insecticides kill friendly insects, so only use them sparingly, after other methods of control have failed.

In a booklet of this size it is only possible to take a look at the more devastating pests and diseases which the gardener has to deal with.

Slugs

Slugs present a problem in every garden and can do great damage to crops and flowers. There is nothing more disheartening to the vegetable gardener than to have a fine row of lettuce plants just coming through the soil, only to be swallowed up by hungry slugs. My one and only complaint about organic gardening is that a mulch of compost over the surface of the soil does tend to encourage slugs. Glow-worms were considered wonderful for controlling the slug. They are hard to find nowadays and may be extinct. A good slug trap is a small container sunk into the soil at surface level and filled with a mixture of milk and water. Slugs fall in and drown. Fertosan slug destroyer prepared from herbs is perfectly safe for humans, animals and plants. You may also use one part of powdered alum mixed with seven parts of slaked lime scattered over the surface of the soil—this proves an effective killer.

Hard working hedgehogs living entirely on insects deserve a place in every garden. They are the finest slug destroyers known and also consume black millipedes, which cause extensive damage. Hedgehogs, unlike birds, will not eat fruit or vegetables and they leave undisturbed all the gardener's friends, including the remarkable little ladybird. If a hedgehog appears in your garden, leave milk for it and you will encourage a faithful worker to stay. The motor car is the biggest threat to the hedgehog. For many years toads and frogs acted as a fine means of control; it is becoming increasingly difficult to find any of these friends of the gardener, they are rapidly dying out in this chemical age. Slugs play a part in the garden in being one of the greatest scavengers, so a measure of control over them is far better than total extinction.

Wireworms

These pests are very active in new gardens or on sites which have not been cultivated for long periods. They will quickly ruin an entire crop of potatoes. Naphthalene flake is a good remedy against wireworms. Traps can easily be set by putting potatoes below the soil on sticks. On being withdrawn weekly, the potatoes will be full of wireworms, thus many can be destroyed before the crop is planted.

Clubroot

This disease goes back beyond the thirteenth century. It is difficult to deal with effectively and rigid crop rotation and liming of soils are good preventive measures. On badly diseased soils all plants of the cabbage family should not be grown for some years. The gardener should also refrain from planting wallflowers, candytuft, nasturtiums and stocks. In the booklet, *Pest Control Without Poisons*, written by Lawrence D. Hills, of The Henry Doubleday Research Centre, experiences of a gardener are given in combating club root. This showed that by putting four pieces of rhubarb, each about 1½ inches in length, into every planting hole for the cabbage or other vegetable, a crop ninety per cent free of clubroot was grown. I've tried this method for many years using only one piece of rhubarb with fifty to seventy-five per cent success, but in future on clubroot infested soils I will take advice from our friend and try using four pieces of rhubarb.

Aphids or Blackfly

Blackfly is a menace that will soon smother a crop of broad beans spreading to spinach and other vegetables, besides invading the flower garden. The writer grows broad beans successfully and rarely resorts to using even an organic insecticide. If an early variety of seed is obtained, they should be sown in boxes or pots in October or November and from such sowings some beans can be gathered before the blackfly appears. Ants herd blackfly like cattle, taking them on the beans to seek the honeydew they secrete. A study of the plants will show the ants being very active before the blackfly appears. So it is essential that your crops of beans are not planted near an ant nest. If tansy is planted nearby it will be effective in keeping the ants away. Flower tips should be pinched out when the beans reach a height of about 18 inches and you will soon be gathering young tasty beans early in the year. Eventually, when the blackfly does appear, ruthlessly cut away all infected parts of the plants. They are tough plants and such cutting does no harm and even promotes further growth. Finally, if necessary, you may resort to using an organic insecticide.

An efficient and safe method of controlling aphids or blackfly is to spray with a solution of soap suds or tobacco water. Plants should be rinsed afterwards.

There are many varied friendly predators and parasites and in a book of this size it is only possible to mention a few. For a better insight into this fascinating subject I would like to refer the reader to *Biological Pest Control Reports* published in interesting little booklets for the price of 3s. 6d. (cheaper to members), written by Lawrence D. Hills, of The Henry Doubleday Research Association, 20, Convent Lane, Bocking, Braintree, Essex.

CHAPTER SEVEN

CHEMICAL FARMING

THE DUST BOWLS of U.S.A., Africa, and Australia are undisputed testimony to the dangers of intensive artificial fertilizing, and chemical farming over a long period. The most successful (and later famous) advocator of organic farming, Sir Albert Howard, mycologist and lecturer on this vital subject, did more to further the cause of natural husbandry than anyone. He farmed at Indore, in India, and introduced the 'Indore Method' of composting. Local organic farming practised by Indian farmers for generations was accepted by Sir Albert. Everything that came out of the soil was returned to it, resulting in wonderful health-giving organic crops. Livestock fed and reared on the produce of organic husbandry became, as the fodder they ate, vital, healthy, free from and able to resist infection, including the dreaded foot-and-mouth disease, in spite of being brought into contact with infected herds. So it is with human beings; we become what we eat. Fresh vegetables and crops grown under natural conditions will make for robust, healthy people, free from many of the ills our present day civilization has brought.

World Wide

Chemical farming spread in America and Europe and other countries have turned away from natural farming. Certain devoted farmers prophesied that prolonged use of artificial fertilizers and insecticides would bring disaster and pave the way for plagues of insects and diseases. Crops would become devitalized, less able to resist disease. Humans and animals, fed entirely on such produce, would suffer in the same way. At the root of many of these grave problems there is one major cause—a sick soil. Artificials will produce large crops, but take much from the soil, whereas natural composting increases humus and fertility. Our garden soil, nurseries, and most important, farmland, must be made so fertile that chemical additives will not be needed.

More and More Chemicals

An interesting insight into the problems of chemical insecticides is given by Rachel Carson in her book, *Silent Spring*, which became a best seller in 1962. Two hundred basic chemicals in the form of sprays, dusts and aerosols were produced for pest and weed control, within the space of twenty-two years. The tragedy is that chemicals exterminate all forms of life, good and bad. But nature likewise turns to war, resulting in pests appearing with a resistance to the poisons. Therefore, stronger, more lethal chemical aids have to be found all the time. Control is vital, but not this vicious circle. The worst aspect is the indiscriminate use of insecticides, which build up in the soil, and in the bodies of animals and humans alike. Before World War II chemicals were obtained from natural sources of minerals and plants—pryrethrum from chrysanthemums, nicotine sulphate from tobacco plants.

Miss Carson mentions the fact that almost the entire bee population perished as a result of arsenic spraying in the cotton growing areas of South U.S.A.

The Torrey Canyon

The wreck of the giant 220,000 ton tanker Torrey Canyon off the Scilly Isles in March, 1967, presented a major problem, with beaches covered in oil. The chemical industry came to the rescue, and tons of detergent were pumped on to the beaches with effective results. However, the clean beaches are sadly lacking in wildlife. Those unfortunate creatures which were not victims of the ghastly oil were killed or badly burned or poisoned by the detergents. Experts are convinced that the effects of the detergent were, in fact, more destructive to wildlife than the oil would have been if left to the elements for dispersal. In France, only beaches used by holiday makers were sprayed, other parts not easily reached were left.

Dangers of Insecticides

Agricultural scientists cannot dispute the destruction of millions of fish in the river Rhine in 1969. The Dutch Health Ministry named the poison as Endosulvan, a powerful insecticide. As a result, over one thousand tons of dead fish were recovered along a three hundred mile stretch of the river in Germany and Holland. Water supplies were cut off from the main cities in Holland. Dutch scientists gave an assurance that the total insecticide in the river was too small to present a health hazard to humans or animals. They may not be so lucky next time. There is no cause for complacency, for the German Government admitted that the entire fish population of the river had been destroyed at a cost of over £300,000. It will be years before fish are plentiful in the Rhine again. So insecticides can really work—with terrible results against the best interests of everyone.

There was the tragic case of Mr. Garner, a keen gardener, who also brewed home-made beer. After drinking a mouthful of weedkiller in mistake for beer, he died three weeks later in hospital. The weedkiller and beer had all been stored in lemonade bottles.

Another instance was of a teenage boy, who drank insecticide in mistake for lemonade. His lungs were extensively burnt, and in spite of a grafting he died.

Poisoned Potatoes

After a farmer sprayed a crop of potatoes to burn off the foliage, to facilitate lifting, a quantity were stolen. In all, 27 people received hospital treatment, and 11 of them were detained for observation, after becoming poisoned through eating poisoned potatoes. Yet another case where an insecticide did more harm than good. The farmer explained that the crops should not have been consumed till 18 days after the spraying.

Loch Leven

The once beautiful Loch Leven, in Scotland, is now dead, following the use of chemical fertilizers and powerful insecticides in the area for decades. By 1967 this lovely lake, at one time teeming with fish, including salmon, became so polluted that all forms of life ceased. Once again we can see for ourselves the results of intensive chemical farming. Raymond Baxter's B.B.C. television film in *Tomorrow's World* on 13th January, 1970, portrayed the full story of the destruction of the Loch very vividly.

D.D.T.

Paul Hermann Muller (1899–1965) a Swiss chemist, was awarded the 1948 Nobel Prize for his discovery of the use of D.D.T. as an insecticide. Everywhere farmers proclaimed it as a godsend in combating insect-borne diseases, saving crops, and preventing starvation. It became famous after World War II, and was used on the population and prisoners to combat lice. D.D.T., once thought to be one of the greatest aids to man, is now known to be dangerous to humans, animals, and our wonderful soil.

Pending Doom

Events which took place in 1969 made history when astronauts walked on the moon. Yet on 1st and 2nd December, 1969, the *Daily Sketch* printed two rather spine-chilling articles. The author, Professor Paul Ehrich, Stanford University, California, U.S.A., claimed that time is running out and, for the world to survive another decade, drastic control of population, chemical insecticides, and pollution will have to be enforced. Concerning chemicals, Professor Ehrich blames D.D.T. and other hydro-carbons as being the most dangerous.

Banning of D.D.T.

Better news for 1969 included an announcement that the U.S.A. will ban the use of D.D.T. within the next two years. This followed the report of a medical panel which also condemned other chemicals as contaminating the environment, including aldrin, dieldrin, endrin, heptachlor, chlordane, benzene-hexachloride, lindane, plus compounds containing arsenic, lead or mercury.

Other countries likewise are beginning to outlaw D.D.T. Canada put rigid restrictions on the use of this chemical. In England, senior Government scientific advisers recommend rigid control of D.D.T. and nine other persistent chemicals for use on the land; these, including D.D.T., will be phased out.

Prince Philip, President, World Wild Life Fund, had this to record in the fund's magazine: 'It is quite easy to justify the use of certain pesticides on the basis that extra food is needed by the starving populations of the world. But is this justification entirely valid, if the long-term side effects of those pesticides destroy whole populations of wild creatures and in the end threaten the health of more people than they save?'

The British Government have now appointed a senior minister as 'Clean-up' overlord to fight pollution in every possible way.

The Vineyards of California

If some readers still have doubts about the dangers of insecticides they may be convinced by events in the vineyards of California. For five years grape pickers have been on strike. Conditions under which Mexican immigrants work are deplorable but the worst aspect concerns insecticides. From 774 workers examined only 121 showed no symptoms of pesticide poisoning. More than 30 different insecticides are used in the vineyards. Some of the unfortunate victims of chemical sprays had lost hair and finger nails. A three year-old child died after sucking his finger, which he had dipped into a container of T.E.P.P., (a chemical spray). A pilot made a forced landing whilst spraying with T.E.P.P.—he was covered in the powder, and soon afterwards became sick and died. Although D.D.T. is being phased out after being used for some ten years, workers are convinced that other equally potent poisons will be introduced into the vineyards. (Thirty years ago, before pesticides were used, biological control was effective in the vineyards by using ladybirds). The effect on wild life in the area is even worse, but the most remarkable thing is that the pests which the poisons have been introduced to kill have a remarkable survival rate. Unfortunately, the friendly insects like ladybirds have mostly been killed off, so the vicious circle continues.

CHAPTER EIGHT

ORGANIC FARMING AND GARDENING ASSOCIATIONS

The Soil Association

THIS MOVEMENT IS an exciting long-term project for investigating the question of organic farming in relation to nutrition and health. In 1945 about one hundred people formed the Soil Association, which now has members in 69 countries.

History of the Farms

Lady Balfour and a Miss Debenham, being deeply concerned about chemical farming, founded the Haughley Research Farms, consisting of New Bells and Walnut Tree farms, the latter becoming the headquarters of the Association. Lady Balfour's book *The Living Soil* became a best seller and caused people to study the vital problem of a world-wide change from organic to chemical farming.

Such a worthwhile movement as The Soil Association exists as a charity, and is registered as such. However, there are signs that people are beginning to wake up to the menace of dangerous insecticides. Many countries are banning such persistent chemicals as D.D.T.

Conversion of Farmland

In 1967 The Pye Trust added Haugh and Brown Street farms to the association and they are being used to show ways of converting monocultural orthodox farmland into flourishing organic husbandry. This is vital for England's agriculture and will show farmers everywhere the merits of organic culture.

It has taken a long time for chemical farming to become widespread and organic methods must be shown to succeed and produce good crops. A sick soil can be made vital, organic, full of humus, but this cannot be achieved overnight. So the work of The Pye Trust in showing how farms can be restored, is the most exciting farming experiment ever. Preserving and keeping the soil in a fine organic state is the birthright of all men. World-wide associations exist to further this worthwhile cause.

The Soil Association's Farms

There are 216 acres of land in three sections split up into organic, mixed and stockless farms. Crops are grown on the organic section and the seed kept for successive years. Livestock consists of cattle, ewes, and poultry. Compost in the form of farmyard manure and vegetable wastes are used on the section. No sprays or fertilizers are employed.

Mixed Section

Very similar to the organic one for livestock and crops, except that the manure from this farm is supplemented by fertilizers, and sprays are used to kill weeds and pests.

Stockless Section (no livestock)

Crops are grown but the only source of organic matter is what remains over from the crops. Artificial fertilizers and sprays are used.

Of the three methods, the organic section is the most self-contained, whereas the mixed section was like the average farm at the time the experiment started. The stockless section comprises a farm without animal manure, a method adopted frequently today.

By these varied systems of agriculture an extensive study is made of the nutritional cycle involving Soil—Plant—Animal—Man.

The 80 acres of the Haugh farm is gradually being changed over to organic farming methods. This is a vital undertaking producing a blueprint for farmers who want to get the best from the land by converting to a natural organic state of husbandry. Brown Street farm (60 acres) is being dealt with in the same manner as Haugh farm.

The Wessex Market Garden

Comprising pig unit and Dutch greenhouses with 20 acres of commercial organic crops, utilized for investigating municipal composting.

The Haughley Market Garden

Eight acres and two large greenhouses are used for commercial and organic cultivation.

Oxerfield Cottage Garden

Laid out as an organic cultivation for the past twenty years, most interesting for all organic gardeners or those converting to natural methods of gardening.

The Association is also making a study of the following:

Radioactive Fallout To determine the amount of radioactive build-up in foods under different cropping systems. Manchester University is assisting with this project.

Natural Control of Insects and Pests This undertaking has been given a grant from the National Environment Research Council.

Microbiological Survey A complicated procedure, dealt with in stages, concerning nutrients in the soil for crops and how they are affected by microbes. Project being controlled by the University of East Anglia.

Municipal Composting Investigation into the toxic hazards of municipal composting, a vital question for thousands of gardeners and allotment holders. University of Birmingham is assisting this project.

A quarterly journal, monthly news sheet, extensive book list and pamphlets on agriculture, gardening, food, health and related subjects are supplied to members. Press conferences, lectures and discussions are held. All this for a membership of £3 per year with special terms for students.

Henry Doubleday

Henry Doubleday, born in 1813, was a Quaker smallholder

who devoted his life to trying to solve the problems of hunger. He believed that Russian comfrey, which he introduced to England, was the crop which could solve starvation. Doubleday gave much to organic gardening and founded the association, which will bear his name as long as organic gardeners till the soil.

Henry Doubleday Research Association

Like the Soil Association, this movement relies on subscriptions from members, which now number some 1,600 in over thirty different countries. Membership ranges from amateur gardeners to Doctors of Philosophy.

News letters have been issued for over eleven years, constituting a unique record of organic gardening in all its aspects. Booklets are available and leaflets are sent out to members (entirely free) covering a very wide range of subjects on natural cultivation. Advice on questions relating to organic gardening is free to members. The expert knowledge of a scientist, professional analyst, mycologist, biologist, and even an entomologist, is available.

Comfrey

Comfrey plants are cultivated and sold in small or large quantities. Comfrey has a wide range of usage including green manure for human consumption and medicinal purposes. Varieties are grown for rabbits, poultry, stockfeed and compost. Research into the medical uses of comfrey is carried out with the help of many medically qualified members. Comfrey ointment is effective for a number of skin complaints. Comfrey tea appears to alleviate arthritis.

Trial Ground

The association has 2 acres of land at Bocking, Essex. This site consists of 25 plots. Different crops are grown and experiments carried out into all aspects of organic gardening.

The Wholefood Finder

Described as being the A.A. book of organic gardening, it contains details of wholefood shops, organic farmers and market gardeners selling direct to the public. All hotels and boarding houses that cultivate their own produce organically or purchase it from other growers, are listed.

The Horticultural Training Centre

Organic gardening has at long last received the recognition it deserves by the formation of The Horticultural Training Centre in conjunction with The Good Gardeners Association at Arkley, Nr. Barnett, Herts. (The association is described at the end of Chapter 3). Courses lasting one and two years (full time) in organic husbandry are offered to students at the centre. Successful students are awarded the General Certificate of the Horticultural Training College.

New Zealand

The Organic Compost Society of New Zealand[1] was formed in 1941, being the oldest movement of this kind on record. A publication, *Soil & Health* is issued with the slogan: 'healthy soil, healthy food, healthy people'. The New Zealanders also have the largest organic gardening society in the world. Dr. Chapman started the movement and by the Society's twenty-first anniversary there were nineteen branches.

The economy of New Zealand has always been related to farming but the pioneers of composting and organic gardening were at first considered cranks. However, with the reputation of Sir Albert Howard behind them, and aided by the devotion of others, the work prospered and organic gardening became accepted as a vital part of horticulture and farming practice. In New Zealand it is estimated that the weight of worms per acre, on sheep pasture, exceeds the weight of the grazing sheep. This country likewise became a leading authority in municipal composting, the art of salvaging and returning all organic wastes to the land. The first plant was put into operation in Auckland in 1948 and it showed that this form of composting

---

[1] Recently renamed The Soil Association

was economical and much organic waste could be recovered and returned to the soil.

Australia

The Organic Farming and Gardening Society of Australia, based on Sir Albert Howard's teachings, bears an emblem in the form of a key, the motto being, 'Healthy soil is the key to good health'. Very true, but nowadays much ignored. A magazine, *Good Earth*, is published and sent free to members.

America

Chemical farming has had devastating effects on large tracts of American farmland. Credit for the success of organic husbandry in America goes to the late Sir Albert Howard. One of Sir Albert's most ardent followers was Mr J. I. Rodale, who pioneered the cause of organic farming.

An important event in the life of Sir Albert was the publishing of his book, *An Agriculture Testament*. He criticized chemical farming and advocated a return to time-proved organic composting. Mr. Rodale was so impressed by this book that he decided to purchase a farm and put the advice into practice. In 1942 the first issue of *Organic Gardening and Farming* was published by Rodale. A life-long friendship developed between Mr. Rodale and Sir Albert Howard.

In 1941 Mr. Rodale took over his farm at Emmaus, Pennsylvania, and was not dismayed at the neglected state in which he found it. He knew from experience of organic husbandry that it would respond to composting and natural cultivation, and he gradually brought the farmland back to a vital 'living soil'.

The farm has a number of experimental plots and both chemical and organic farming is carried out and comparisons made. In nearly all cases the organic methods of cultivation have been shown to be superior.

The vital work carried out by Mr. Rodale on his farm is only part of this interesting story. He was a man of great energy and resources who wrote many books. Further, in addition to

Organic Gardening and Farming, he initiated *Prevention*, and *Health Bulletin*. These journals have a world-wide circulation.

Canada

In Canada a movement exists called 'Land Fellowship', counterpart of The Soil Association in England. Canadian farmers, members of The Land Fellowship, concerned about chemical farming, adopt less spectacular methods of pest control, reporting excellent results from organic farming.

Worms Galore

Dr. Grussendorf, a Canadian organic gardener, noted that worms were slow to invade the centre of his compost heaps. He bred a new hybrid strain of worm which is very prolific and active in the compost heap. When a heap is being built, he spreads a few worms around the base. These rapidly penetrate the centre and when the heap is opened up, top and contents are alive with masses of active worms. The writer can vouch for this healthy sign, which has taken place in compost heaps he has made for over fifteen years.

Another Canadian, Hans Birk, achieved remarkable results by using the earthworm for organic gardening. He eventually went into business breeding worms, which he sent to organic gardeners in many countries.

Switzerland

The Swiss are making tremendous progress in going 'back to nature' on their farms. Switzerland is the birthplace of a process known as 'Natural Biological Farming'. Six hundred commercial co-operative Swiss farmers changed to organic husbandry eight years ago. They farm without fertilizers or chemical insecticides. They are also experts in the art of biological control. An example of this is, that in order to overcome the devastating red spider mite on cucumbers, they use the South African tick beetle which devours red spider mites as fast as they breed, but hates cucumbers. So the Swiss farmer produces organically grown cucumbers and other crops free from poisonous insecticides. It seems unbelievable that D.D.T. was discovered in Switzerland and the country still produces and exports large quantities of insecticides, artificial fertilizers, pesticides and other chemicals, which do not seem to find a place on their own farms!

South Africa

Credit for The Organic Soil Association of South Africa goes to Dr. Robert McKibbin. He always remembered a heart-rendering experience when he was four years old. Robert and his brother had been presented with a pair of baby rabbits, but their happiness was short lived; within a week both rabbits were dead. A post mortem showed that they had been poisoned from an insecticide dusted on the carrot tops which they had eaten. This incident paved the way for Dr. McKibbin to form the association, for the tragic death of the rabbits was never forgotten. Dr. McKibbin followed the work of Sir Albert Howard, whose timely advice and vast experience saved the banana crops of many American Republics. The growers were desperate and the economy of many parts was in the balance. Acting on the advice of Sir Albert, the crops were not only saved but organic farming was introduced, which resulted in bigger and better yields of fruit in soils almost free from devastating pests and diseases. Dr. McKibbin was so impressed with these events that he wrote to the editor of the Soil Association magazine in America, expressing his thanks for the excellent advice regarding the dangers of chemical farming, and the manner in which Sir Albert Howard's system had overcome them. To his surprise, Sir Albert replied in person, and a life-long contact with regular correspondence developed between them.

The present Organic Soil Association of South Africa has two Garden Clubs and a Health Group. A journal entitled, *Soil Sense* is published.

Conclusion

The average person is just not prepared to accept organic gardening and farming and, like herbal medicine, it is considered by many to be outdated. European Conservation Year and the problems of pollution will help overcome prejudice. However, only when organic gardening has its own journal to take a place on bookstalls together with other gardening magazines will it be more widely accepted.